Animal Teams

Ant Colonies

by Matt Lilley

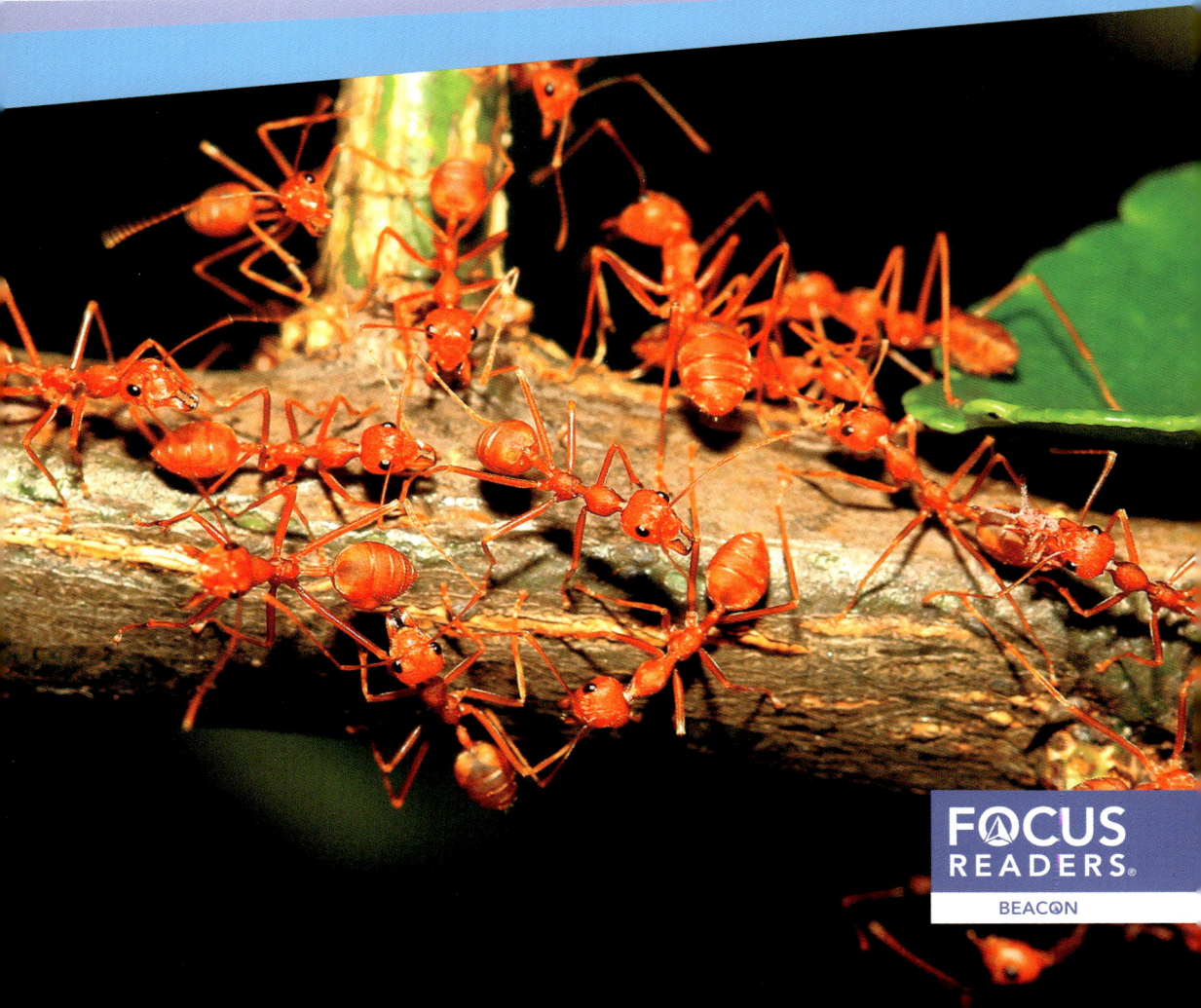

FOCUS READERS

BEACON

www.focusreaders.com

Focus Readers is distributed by North Star Editions:
sales@northstareditions.com | 888-417-0195

Produced for Focus Readers by Red Line Editorial.

Photographs ©: Shutterstock Images, cover, 1, 8, 10, 12, 14, 17, 19, 20–21, 22, 25, 27, 28–29; iStockphoto, 4; Clay Coleman/Science Source, 6

Library of Congress Cataloging-in-Publication Data
Names: Lilley, Matt, author.
Title: Ant colonies / by Matt Lilley.
Description: Mendota Heights, MN : Focus Readers, [2025] | Series: Animal
  teams | Includes bibliographical references and index. | Audience:
  Grades 2-3
Identifiers: LCCN 2023050729 (print) | LCCN 2023050730 (ebook) | ISBN
  9798889981886 (hardcover) | ISBN 9798889982449 (paperback) | ISBN
  9798889983538 (pdf) | ISBN 9798889983002 (ebook)
Subjects: LCSH: Ants--Juvenile literature. | Ants--Behavior--Juvenile
  literature. | Ant communities--Juvenile literature.
Classification: LCC QL568.F7 L55 2025 (print) | LCC QL568.F7 (ebook) |
  DDC 595.79/6--dc23/eng/20231204
LC record available at https://lccn.loc.gov/2023050729
LC ebook record available at https://lccn.loc.gov/2023050730

Printed in the United States of America
Mankato, MN
082024

About the Author

Matt Lilley has written more than 20 nonfiction children's books. He also has an MS in scientific and technical writing. The focus of his degree was on health writing for kids. He loves researching and writing about all sorts of topics. He lives in Minnesota with his family.

Table of Contents

Chapter 1

Escaping a Flood

Rain pours from the sky. The ground begins to flood. Inside an anthill, tunnels fill with water. Fire ants rush to escape. The worker ants collect eggs. They hurry to grab the young ants, too.

Ants have hard outer shells that help them stay dry in the rain.

Ants in a raft keep changing places so no ant stays underwater for too long.

The workers carry them up to the surface. The queen comes as well. Then the workers gather in a group.

They link their legs together. Their bodies make a raft. The water rises around them. But the ants float.

Later, the ant-raft reaches dry land. Scouts leave the raft and look around. They find a good place for a nest. Workers let down the queen, eggs, and young ants. It's time to build their new nest.

Did You Know?

Fire ants are the only kind of ant that makes rafts.

Chapter 2

The Queen and Her Colony

Ants live in **colonies**. Each ant has a specific role. But they all work together. That way, they can work faster. And they can do things that one ant could not do alone.

▷ **Some anthills can be several feet tall.**

The most important member of the colony is the queen. She lays the eggs. That keeps the colony going. When a queen is born, she is different from regular **larva**. She has a special **gene**. The other ants feed her more food. That helps her grow into a queen.

Later, the queen's wings grow. She flies away from her colony. Male ants also leave the colony at this time. The males are called drones. The queen **mates** with them.

Then the queen starts looking for a place to begin a new colony. This process can be very dangerous. That's because the queen is alone.

A weaver ant queen sits with her eggs.

She has no food. Also, she must avoid **predators**. She needs to find somewhere safe. When the queen

12

finally settles, she lays her first eggs. The new colony has begun.

Over time, the queen lays more and more eggs. She can lay 800 a day. Some of the eggs become male drones. But most will be worker ants. All the workers are females. These ants do the tasks that keep the colony going.

Did You Know?

After mating, male drones die. Their only job is done.

Chapter 3

The Workers

Running a colony is hard work. Sometimes the queen needs to be fed. Tunnels need to be dug. The new larvae need attention. Worker ants take care of all these jobs.

➤ Larvae rely on workers to feed them before they grow into adult ants.

They do most other tasks around the nest, too.

Workers have different roles over time. When they are young, they do safe jobs. They take care of younger ants. They build and fix the nest. They stay inside.

When workers are older, their jobs get more dangerous. They fight off intruders. They also leave the nest to find food. Gathering enough food for the nest is hard work. So, an ant might leave a scent trail. Other ants

follow the trail to the food. Then, many ants work together to carry the food home.

Workers do other jobs together outside the nest, too. Some join their bodies. They build bridges.

That helps them cross gaps. Some ants help one another lift things.

Many types of ants have **specialized** workers. Leafcutter ants come in different sizes. The biggest have huge heads. They protect the nest. Medium-size leafcutters use their jaws to cut

18

▷ **Leafcutter ants carry pieces of leaves they collected.**

leaves. The smallest ants ride on the leaves. They protect the bigger ants from flies. Each job is important.

Aphid Farming

Aphids are tiny insects. They use sap from plants to make honeydew. Honeydew is a sweet liquid. Ants drink it.

To get more honeydew, some ants herd aphids. They carry the aphids onto plants. They protect the aphids from predators. At night, they even carry the aphids into the nest.

If the ant colony moves, the ants carry aphid eggs with them. At the new nest, they start a new herd. That way, the ants always have enough honeydew.

An ant walks along a stem covered in aphids.

Chapter 4

Communication

To work together, ants need strong **communication**. Ants use movement and sound to communicate. Some ants have spikes on their bodies. An ant can rub its spike with its legs.

> Ant bodies have three main parts. Each ant has a head, thorax, and abdomen.

The rubbing lets out a sound. It lets other ants know that help is needed.

Ants use smell as their main form of communication. Ants have **glands** all over their bodies. These glands make **chemicals**. Each chemical has a scent with a different meaning. For example, some scents show where food is. Other ants can smell the chemicals through their **antennae**. They understand the message.

▶ **A group of small black ants try to attack a larger ant.**

Some scents let ants know when to attack. When ants fight, they might get injured. So, ants also have a scent to tell others they are hurt. Other ants can carry them to safety.

Ants also know one another by their smells. Each colony has its own scent. Sometimes a strange ant comes close to a colony. If the ant doesn't smell right, ants from the colony might attack. Workers with different jobs can also have

A weaver ant carries away a dead ant.

different scents. That way, ants can know each other's job.

When an ant dies, its scent changes. The other ants notice. Workers carry away the dead ant. A new ant takes its place. The colony can continue working.

FOCUS ON
Ant Colonies

Write your answers on a separate piece of paper.

1. Write a few sentences describing different jobs that worker ants do.

2. If you were an ant, would you want to be a queen, drone, or worker? Why?

3. Which kind of ant can form a raft?
   - A. fire ant
   - B. leafcutter ant
   - C. honeypot ant

4. What would happen if a worker ant were separated from its colony?
   - A. It would start a new colony.
   - B. It would join a different colony.
   - C. It would either find its colony or die.

5. What does **scouts** mean in this book?

*Later, the ant-raft reaches dry land. **Scouts** leave the raft and look around. They find a good place for a nest.*

    A. ants that search for something
    B. ants that make rafts
    C. ants that sleep

6. What does **intruders** mean in this book?

*When workers are older, their jobs get more dangerous. They fight off **intruders**.*

    A. ants that bring food to a colony
    B. ants that attack a colony
    C. ants that clean a colony

Answer key on page 32.

Glossary

antennae
Long, skinny organs on the heads of insects.

chemicals
Specific kinds of matter. Some chemicals can be harmful, and some can be helpful.

colonies
Groups of animals that live together.

communication
The process of giving and receiving information.

gene
A tiny part of a cell that causes the body to develop certain traits.

glands
Organs in the body that produce chemicals used by other parts of the body.

larva
An insect that has hatched from an egg and is in the early stages of life.

mates
Comes together in order to have babies.

predators
Animals that hunt other animals for food.

specialized
Involved in a particular type of activity.

To Learn More

BOOKS

French, Jess. *The Book of Brilliant Bugs*. New York: DK Publishing, 2020.

Owen, Ruth. *Leafcutter Ants*. Minneapolis, Lerner Publishing, 2021.

Pallotta, Jerry. *Green Ants vs. Army Ants*. Minneapolis: Abdo Publishing, 2024.

NOTE TO EDUCATORS

Visit **www.focusreaders.com** to find lesson plans, activities, links, and other resources related to this title.

Index

A
antennae, 24
aphids, 20

C
chemicals, 24–27
communication, 23–27

D
drones, 11, 13

E
eggs, 5, 7, 10, 13, 20

F
fighting, 16, 25
fire ants, 5–7
food, 11–12, 16–17,
   20, 24

H
honeypot ants, 18

L
larva, 10, 15
leafcutter ants, 18–19

P
predators, 12, 20

Q
queen, 6–7, 10–13, 15

W
worker ants, 5–7, 13,
   15–19, 26–27